Seven Steps to Joy

a life changing path

ANTONELLA LO RE

POWER HOUSE
PUBLISHING

ALEXANDRIA
VIRGINIA

Seven Steps To Joy
A Life Changing Path

by Antonella Lo Re

Published by:
Powerhouse Publishing
625 N. Washington Street, Suite 425
Alexandria, Virginia 22314

info@powerhousepublishing.net
703-982-0984

Copyright ©2017 Antonella Lo Re

All rights reserved. No part of this book may be reproduced in any form or by any means electronic or mechanical including but not limited to photocopying, recording, or by any information storage and retrieval system without written permission from the authors except for the inclusion of brief quotations in a review.

ISBN First Paperback Edition: 1976563038

First paperback printing October 2017

Lo Re, Antonella
Seven steps to joy, a life changing path
1st paperback ed.

ISBN-10: 1976563038
ISBN-13: 978-1976563034

TABLE OF CONTENTS

Acknowledgements...................................5

Introduction.......................................7

Chapter 1   Growing up or Growing old................11

Chapter 2   Step One: Love...........................17

Chapter 3   Step Two: Forgiveness 29

Chapter 4   Step Three: Compassion...................35

Chapter 5   Step Four: Gratitude.....................39

Chapter 6   Step Five: Acceptance....................45

Chapter 7   Step Six: Silence........................51

Chapter 8   Step Seven: Trust 57

Chapter 9   The path to joy..........................61

Chapter 10 Finding Your Purpose Through Intuition 69

Chapter 11 Epilogue.................................79

Resources..83

Endnotes...85

ACKNOWLEDGMENTS

I would like to acknowledge and firstly thank my daughter Emma. While I was teaching her how to hold a spoon and fork and how to walk, she taught me about unconditional love, she has been my light, my hope, and my motivation.

I wish to express the deepest love for my dear husband, Maurizio, who passed away only few months ago after a dreadful illness and immense suffering. He made me promise that I would put this book out into the world after having finished writing it at the end of 2014. He taught me curiosity for life, generosity for the world, thirst for knowledge, and a great sense of compassion.

I thank, my mother and father for putting me into this world and for teaching me discipline.

I cannot forget here two of my dearest friends Daniela and Martina who have not only encouraged me, but "requested" to put these words on paper for years.

I thank all those friends that have also demonstrated unconditional love throughout decades of friendship even while hardship came along, they encouraged me to be a better me.

I am also thanking those who told me I would have never made it in life, that my worth was not enough to achieve and accomplish any of my dreams. They hurt me, but in the long run I understood that it was only about them, they brought out the strong desire to lift myself up again after reaching rock bottom. They taught me how not to be like them and how to work within myself to get rid of that dynamite of anger within that could explode any time for no reason like theirs. They taught me how to search for different patterns and choose instead to search for loving and compassionate attitude towards life and towards others.

I thank those I forgave and I thank all those I would like to be forgiven by. They are all part of this journey that conducted me here.

I thank the Universe, God and the Higher Source, for giving me the privileges I have had throughout my life, this wonderful journey. I had opportunities to choose to grow up not only grow old.

Thank you.

INTRODUCTION

Joy is the lost gift we are self-condemned to search for, all while having it within ourselves. We are so distracted and defocused from ourselves that we go around running endlessly in the hamster wheel until we exhaust ourselves, sadly missing it.

Joy is something we are born with and is easy to find. For example, observe babies, they do not need things to smile and be happy; they have no fears and no anxiety. Unfortunately, we step in to spoil a great deal of this innate joy. We teach children how to be unhappy convincing them they will be happy only if they acquire things, if they are able to be first in class, if they look smarter than others, or if they get the best score in their fitness contest. We are so good at derailing them from looking within, that we dread if a child tells us he or she is bored. Boredom is a good thing, it can help them to connect with their own Self. It can lead them to listen to themselves and learn how to be and not only to do. Why are we so scared of that? After doing a great job deceiving them and often realizing that the results are not really what we hoped for, we suggest them to go on spiritual retreats and we might ask for a loan to pay for it. They must go to these self-development retreats or to countries where they can touch and feel, for fifteen days in their lives, the reality of children that exist and can be even happy without one-fourth of what they have. But they must go there to find themselves!

In the meantime, we have become so wise that we cannot wait to teach them what we have just learned in only our last session of the same retreats we highly recommend. We can hardly contain the enthusiasm because, truly, we are very happy that we could for once got off the hamster wheel and understand what's going on within us even for a short while. We are looking forward to "teaching" and sharing the little we got to know. We feel that now we have the magic formula for a happy life and for reaching the sought-after joy, that nothing looks scary anymore. We must be careful though, our ego is deceiving us once again, and it is right in the middle of where it should not be. Let's put it aside for a while and give ourselves the time to process what we've figured out so far and realize that the road ahead is somewhat long or may be even endless. The "process" is a lifelong journey. It is not a destination, it's a voyage.

It is now very common to hear how positive thinking can change our lives. And I am here not to deny that, please keep that in mind. It is common practice now to introduce a great deal of positive affirmations in our daily life as if this Universe is somewhat deaf or has comprehension issues. Repeating the affirmation over and over, declaring to the world what we want, once again, outside of us, ending up wishing our life away. Post-it notes with all of our affirmations and positive thinking even when, for example the awful mother in law has sabotaged the most (and only) romantic moment in the last two decades of your marriage and you really want her to go and live as far away as possible, preferably with no planes for some decades and a limited internet connection few times a year, but we find the positive affirmations and thoughts even for her. "I thank the Universe for giving me her as mother in law instead of a serial killer". Jokes aside, I am not here to deny the power of thoughts, positive thinking and affirmations. I am only here to say that if we rely only on those things, chances are that we end up with our house entirely plastered with post-it notes, the same mother in law and a life that gets wished away.

From personal experience, I believe there are several other issues to face and to work on in order to be in alignment with the Universal Laws. Only then, are we able to receive the response from the Universe and *also* reach that Joy we longed for.

This book encountered you for a reason. Remember though, "It's not what you read, but what you decide to do with what you read, that will make a difference".

This book will help you focus on some essential steps to reach and keep the vibration of joy in your life while walking the highs and lows of your own inner journey. It will help you to re-connect with a state of joy which will not prevent all aspects of life from happening, but it will give you the strength to face it and learn to accept the bumps and sorrows of this life lessons while maintaining a sense of serenity and joy.

If you decide to follow these steps and encompass them with your affirmations and positive thinking practice it will be a life changing path.

CHAPTER 1

GROWING UP OR GROWING OLD

If this book encountered you, it's because you are in a path of awareness. You made the conscious decision that in addition of what you are and what you experience there is more and you are determined to figure out what that is. You are awake, you no longer want to live in a sleep mode. Well, this new look at your existence, your attempts to learn more, your wanting to get some answers to big questions of life make you a seeker. By being a seeker you make the conscious choice of growing up not only old.

The father of western philosophy, Socrates, believed that with wondering starts the walk towards wisdom. Congratulations!

We hear a lot about mindfulness meditation, positive thinking, affirmations, change your thoughts change your life which I believe all being valid, relevant and great tools in support of our inner journey but not the only ones. There is more to it in order to be able to navigate through the rough and harsh times of life. These pages want to point out inner abilities we all have and guide you to work on and practice them to give you what you need to add up to your path of affirmation, positive thinking mindfulness and whatever else you figured out so far.

Before starting with the Seven Steps though, I need to mention the importance of the choice you have made undertaking this journey of yours. You have chosen to live an awakened life which entails to understand and embrace to live in the present moment. The past no longer belongs to us, and the future is not yet ours. To be fully present in what we are doing, or in what we are sharing this moment of life with, is to be awakened. This right moment while your eyes are scrolling down onto these lines is your present, nothing else.

Conversely, choosing not to live an awakened life means that you're only letting time pass by without embracing the bliss of each moment., we waste time wishing for more, wishing for something different, craving a different life that might never happen, and complaining about what we do not have. This stagnancy and lack of acceptance with the present is what I define as "growing old without growing up." It is like moving in a flat and dull circle for years instead of moving up on a spiral which represents our evolution and growth. When we are in that circle, we crave what we do not have, we allow the present moment to pass unnoticed. We only get the fixation of the unknown future and the unknown life, searching for something that we are not even sure we are missing. Therefore, we create our own burden that is making us eternally unhappy and unsatisfied.

A glance at life

If we look retrospectively at our life so far, I am sure we have something in common. Can you recall times when you have stumbled, fallen, reached rock bottom, and suffered the deepest pain you could handle? Take a moment to reflect upon that collective pain and think where you are now, you can probably find relief for being over those dreadful moments of your life you thought would never pass. If you push it a little bit further, I am sure you can even feel some gratitude because you went through that for a reason, "That" was only the path that was able to lead you to where you are today. "That" is what pushed you and me forward. At the time, it was the unknown forward and we could not stand or understand it. We must admit though that even through a painful passage but we did evolve, we did grow up.

Evolution is any process of development or moving forward, and whatever happens in our life, whether good or bad, high or low, it is moving us to where we need to be.

Moments of hardship are scary, draining and tough to handle, but they define changes. Human being does not deal well with changes because our ego wants always certainty while changes are mere un-certainty therefore changes become traumatic and often very painful experiences.

Changes are part of this earthly journey, unavoidable stepping stones for our own path of evolution.

Life *is* change, it is a script we read one line at a time without getting to know or be able to read the line that follows. We need to be prepared like when reading music and playing an instrument to go through its *forte, piano, allegretto, crescendo,* and *diminuendo*. We must learn to dance to life's rhythm, flow with its rhythm, do not become stuck.

We must learn to keep the flow, be the water that flows over, under, or around the stagnant rock, even when it requires embracing an unknown direction.

If we say *"yes"* to life we must learn its music and learn to dance at its rhythm, a rhythm we cannot control though. If we reach the point of knowing how to flow the unknown will no longer scare us, I believe this is the only way we can appreciate life and recognize its wonders. We can embrace it as a wonderful journey where we are actively involved instead of passive viewers sitting on the sidelines waiting for time to pass by.

We all know by experience that the landscape of life changes and manifests different colors. There are occasions when life can be tiring and blue, other times dull and grey, but there will always be a time when life is more pleasant and vibrant.

Each of us has a story inside—a tale to tell, a scar to heal, a pain to reveal. Ultimately, experiencing suffering brings us closer to our Highest Self and centers us in a place of joy and love.

When in the centered condition of joy and love, you do not *need* anything or anyone—not one more thing, one more vacation, or one more friend to please you or give you the long-sought-after "happiness." It's a place of joy, peace, and serenity. This state is a place to understand that life is unfolding before you—accept the events and the occurrences in the present.

Does what I have just said make sense to you? Probably in theory. What to do after understanding this concept intellectually, how can I put this in practice? This is the real challenge I am sure many of you face. I did.

If you chose to undertake your spiritual path you are looking to live through your authentic power you are starting to take responsibility for your own earthly presence.

You have probably felt your guts twisted so brutally that you had no choice but to move on. Yes, it can get so unbearable that you *must* move forward. It is said that sometimes nothing changes until the pain of staying the same is far greater than the pain of changing.

As weird as it sounds, that guts twisting pain is right what conducted you here and what will help you to grow up, not only grow old. Your soul will evolve; your heart will open and probably closing again and again to re-open to another level wisdom. Many of us have turned to a real commitment of changing our thoughts, re-programming our brains, learning to be more positive, more grateful, using positive affirmations to the point that we weaved our bathroom mirrors kitchen counters, office space of colorful post it note with the affirmations we want to engrave inside as deep as possible for them to have the power to change the outcome of our lives. Often, I hear: - "Despite my effort and hard work I put on it for months and years, nothing has changed!"-

This is when I believe a very close look to the seven inner abilities is necessary. Let's have a look at them:

1. Love
2. Forgiveness
3. Compassion
4. Gratitude
5. Acceptance
6. Silence
7. Trust

These crucial inner abilities can guide your life. Whenever this multidimensional world is throwing you off, remind yourself of them. There is only one essential and crucial condition requested when working on each and every of these abilities: keep an open heart.

Learning and applying them is not an overnight process; actually, It's rather a laborious progression. They are a continuous reminder of your focus—where you want to go in your life—and will redirect you toward that goal whenever you fall off track. Living by these inner abilities will make a huge difference in your life and will keep you on a positive path, with your heart open to allow giving, as well receiving.

They will enable your inner growth and evolution therefore transforming your life.

In learning to master them, you will also learn to rely and count on them in order to grow up and evolve rather than only growing old and sadly letting the clock tick your life away. Finally you will be able to take ownership of your own existence and you will look forward to meeting your future!

The next seven chapters explore these inner abilities in great depth and suggest ways to implement them in your life.

CHAPTER 2

STEP ONE: LOVE

> *"Choose love independently from what is happening in your life, or what has happened inside or outside of yourself and around you."*
>
> — *Antonella Lo Re*

Love is a grounding and healing force. Love's energy is the strongest force, it is the essence of life, the primal binding and driving force of the Universe. Its healing energy permeates a being like water does to a riverbank, nourishing the dry soil, giving birth to more life, and allowing expansion of life. Love is a feeling produced by action. When we care, serve, attend, listen, empathize, and sacrifice with true willingness, *we love*. Love comes out of these actions and it does not abide to any condition. If the love you believe to be present is not unconditional, and it fades away, then it is not love.

Nowadays, the word itself is often overused and abused. I believe we came to an inappropriate use of it confusing it with momentary emotions that although strong they are temporary, they come in and carry us in their vortex for a while and then vanish. It does not matter how long, it does not matter the type of relationship whether friendship or romance. Love is an active force, it's not a passive energy simply happening to us therefore, it is not something that fades away it can transform itself, but it cannot fade away.

Love is not possession. It is protection and care, not to be confused with control, sometimes manipulation undercover as "guidance". This is true in any relationship, including the "me relationship". I believe it is necessary to have a closer look at the love in our relationships present in our daily lives: parental love, love for others, love for ourselves.

Parental and filial love

As a young woman, I read *The Prophet*[1] by Khalil Gibran, and the poem about children has then stayed with me since, together with some thoughts by Edward Bach. In the aforementioned poem, Gibran refers to children as "children of life," who do not belong to parents. They are independent thinkers and belong only to themselves. We parents, are only a vehicle to bring them to life, and they are not our possession. Edward Bach speaks about parenthood as an office in life that we have.[2] It's a temporary duty we have in order to offer guidance and protection to our children.

When I first saw Emma, my daughter, I welcomed her into this world. I made a vow to be as good as a mother as I could be to that soul. It was clear to me though that I wanted to stand to her as the bow of the archer is to the arrow—a stable point for her to sprint into her life, to lean on, to take nourishment from. It was my determination to support her and to pass onto her whatever I had for her to take, allowing her to make it hers. This is exactly what I told her when they put her in my arms. She was looking around with big beautiful brown eyes, eager to understand where she was. I was conscious that from that moment onward, that I was the vehicle for her to live her purpose in life. I welcomed her and thanked her for choosing me as that catalyst, and for giving me such a privilege. This was our first communication—my very first "Mom talk". As many of you that experienced parenthood probably have, I noticed that everyday my love for the newborn baby in my arms was growing. I realized the love I had for her when she was first born was not as strong and immense as what I felt two weeks later, three months later, a year later, and so forth. Love is a growing force that nurtures and develops life, it's a growing power weaved into this Universe and from this Universe. Can you, parents, relate?

The reason why I also called this paragraph "filial love" is for those who are reading these lines and are only children, with the hope for them to understand the love our parents have for us. Excessive love can make mistakes too and more than often it tangles with fears and anxiety. All we need to do is to love back and sometimes be able to reassure.

Love and romance

When it comes to romantic relationships, we often confuse love with passion. We treat love as an emotion; we call it "love" when, in reality, we are referring to passion—an intense emotion that can barely be controlled. We have plenty of case studies around us, and most of us I believe, experienced this misunderstanding of love as an integral force. We confuse passion with love in relationships, too often with the result of feeling stranded, lost, disappointed, miserable, exhausted and often time lonely.

Passion starts from where all other emotions start from. If we think of emotions like fear, anxiety, excitement, anger, where do we feel these emotions when they arise? In which part of our body? In the lower belly.

The love I am talking about, instead, is a centered force and it comes from our heart, from our center and from there, it can grow, it can transform, but it will not vanish. When true love is present, there is no attachment, dependence or judgement, no conditions dictated by our ego even if it is its favorite task.

Love in other relationships

As for non-romantic relationships, I invite you to think for a moment of all kind of relationships you have around yourself now. How many are suffering or have suffered for rigidity of the heart by somebody else?

Frequently, very trivial events turn into big reasons to stop our love flow towards somebody and most of the time the effects linger for decades, no matter if the reason was unimportant, maybe a friend expected something from us and we unintentionally forgot? The key to unfreezing that event and free ourselves is love and the access door to it is through our hearts. Only if we are willing to use the flexibility of our heart will we avoid getting stuck in decade-old resentments for some old occurrences of the past.

The heart is the channel, the floodgate through which love flow is possible. If it is closed, it will prevent the passage of love, love will not go out as it will not get in. So how can we get to that place of love? How can we always keep our heart open—even towards whom and what our ego has designated to be "not acceptable" therefore deserving our resentment? We must learn to surrender a challenging task for any of us. It is pretty natural for human beings shutting the floodgate of love when we are hurt, suffer, or when in grief, or simply when we have to deal with emotional baggage. We do enter a defense mode, we chain ourselves for ever to what, we think or to what truly caused our pain; sometimes, living an entire life in this way, whether aware of it or not. This happens because closing our heart may be the only way we know. Living in defense mode enables us to initiate and master a vicious circle of pain, madness and nonsense, derailing us from listening to our true Self. Destined to the only achievement of feeling distressed and enervated, without any sense of direction. The only task left becomes watching the clock ticking your time away, usually feeling very sad, unaccomplished and lonely.

By keeping our heart closed, not only do we prevent love from flowing in and outwards, we also prevent the manifestation of the positive, grandness, and magnificence in store for us to reveal itself. Each and every person has magnificent opportunities and true wonders in his/her own spiritual birth plan. They have been woven into our life's journey, into the tapestry of our existence in this dimension, waiting to be revealed.

Nothing is more devastating than lack of love. Since love is not a unilateral force, but rather it comes in and it goes out in order to be true, it must be given just as much as its reception must be permitted but if the walls are up there is no way in as no way out.

Many of us believe that love must be deserved, therefore we let our mind to do the screening and select who deserves our love and who does not. Many times in my talks I get this observation; "*But*...I got so hurt by such and such..."

The question is not to be hurt or not, or to think to be hurt or not, the true challenge is to avoid falling into self-defense mode and choose the love pathway which will bring us to another level of existence where peace and joy are more of a constant rather than a seldom condition. Whenever I hear: "yes I understand but..." there is already a condition that our mind wants to dictate. It is right here when compassion comes in. Understanding and accepting other's limitations, refraining from judging their doing and staying on our own path of love. That's all I believe is required to keep our heart open. If we are able to love unconditionally we enable ourselves to live in the light, peace and joy. Love is not linked to fairness or unfairness either.

I remember having a conversation with my wise friend and spiritual guide. I went to him, speaking about the unfairness I felt deep in me and the injustice I faced at work: less competent people had obtained better positions and salaries, for example. I asked him how this could happen. Again, his smile was an overture to another "a-ha" moment of mine. At first, I did not understand him at all, and even found his answer annoying. He told me, "You are talking this way because you think of life as unfair. Try to think of it as fair." I left frustrated and absolutely convinced that we were both not even slightly comprehending each other! It dawned on me later to try to apply what he said, and I soon realized what he meant. We are all in this world at a certain phase and stage pertaining only to us. We have a start line and a finish line belonging only and exclusively to us. Whatever we experience or see others experiencing, is what we, or they, need to experience right in that exact moment of their existence. Everything is fair. We only see it as unfair when we take it out of context and place it in our own confining little box designed by our own mind. So, many springs later, I realized that love for others has and *must* have nothing to do with fairness/unfairness, deserving or not deserving.

Love is the ability to listen to others and refrain from judgement, it must be unconditional, if we could only comprehend and learn how to love those who hurt us for whom they are: human beings, rings of this chain of humanity. As we are all interconnected, we are an extension of the Higher Source and we are not separated from each other; therefore, love cannot be confined—limited to some and not others. It is only our mind dictating our aversion towards others giving us a list of who to love or not. There is a kind of love, Universal love, that we must be a conduit for through the chain of beings we are part of and as creatures of love, we have to keep this energy flowing.

Thus, give yourself a new challenge, choose to say, "I love you." Even to those your mind has kicked them out from the good list, love them. The more you love them the more you loosen up the chain that keeps you tied to them to the point you will feel free and you will free them from your life. Little by little it will grow on and in you if you make it a daily practice. It might be hard to do at first, but it will be very rewarding. You will find the progress extremely liberating and will discover you are actually able to say, "I love you" to those people who hurt you. By doing so, it will be clear to us that our love for them is not at all related to their actions towards us, but only and exclusively to their souls, which we will learn to bow to. Since love is not about paying back, but paying forward, do not worry about where the stone you throw into the lake goes. Just throw it and enjoy watching the ripple effect.

To be very frank, I am adamant in emphasizing that this process is not an overnight process, but it can take a *very long* while. It might be even excruciating, at first, to pass through our list and say, "I love you." In the beginning, it might only be a chore based on good intentions. Soon, though, we will own it, each name of our list and each "I love you" makes the communion of souls grow stronger. When we are hurt by these people, and the hurt has stayed close to our soul, performing this exercise, makes the distance between our soul and that hurt grew bigger, our heart becomes lighter, and our life expands, we will start feeling joy flowing in all compartments of our life.

It took me years to understand and *feel* that we truly *are* "love"—this magnificent energy. Loving others and being able to have universal love for everyone, with no distinctions or judgments is a great exercise in daily life. Even if you keep on going back and forth, ebbing and flowing. It may be tangled up with your personal sense and concept of fairness and unfairness, forgiving or forgetting, but at last the gap between you and them will get narrower.

Only when we are able to love freely, no matter who or what, will our resistance cease, our heart will expand, our life will expand, and we will truly love and respect ourselves. Life will have more meaning, and joy will pour onto us. It does take practice, but each time we are able to say "I love you" unconditionally, we will be closer and closer to the best of life. We are participating in this earthly journey to fall apart and be put together repeatedly. The opening and closing of the heart is an unavoidable step in the process of self-improvement.

Love for Yourself

Many years ago, I read a quote that essentially said the real lifelong romance starts when you begin to love yourself. At the time, I thought of how selfish it was and how egocentric would be to apply this principle in my life! Well, now I can tell you that love towards ourselves *is* essential.

I remember talking to my wise friend in a day, at a time when I thought that my giving and receiving where equally balanced. Within minutes, I realized I had very little love for myself. I do recall his compassionate smile and admirable balance he said to me: "Dear, what would you do if a beggar came up to you and asked for the one dollar you had in your pocket?" I replied, "Of course, I would give it to him!" Then he proceeded to ask me,

"What if you had no dollar in your pocket? What would you do?" I stuttered, "Well, I could not give it to him."

He smiled again and warmly said, "Dear, if you do not have love for yourself...that coin in your pocket...how do you plan to give it to someone else?" That was another a-ha moment in my life!

We live in a hectic society. We are so caught up in the "busyness" of life that we walk along, absentmindedly following the tasks we have to accomplish in a day. We let our tasks, jobs, and calendars manage us rather than us manage them. This is seen in how the word "busy" has now replaced the word "fine." It's true…When you ask somebody, "How are you?" You often, too often, get the answer, "Busy." It's apparently the new trend to be busy, and it's not cool at all to be un-busy. We have lost track of many little but significant details and simple and ordinary marvel of each day of our lives that make the true outcome of our lives.

In our frenetic lifestyle, how can we explain and transfer this love towards us? By acknowledging the whole that we are: body, mind, and spirit, and caring for each of them daily. By choosing to have moments that will count as drops of great luxury throughout our day and our week, moments for ourselves. Being in silence, smelling the roses, noticing a sunset, having a tea with a loved one, taking a bath and having a spa meeting with ourselves, reading a favorite poem, listening to soul-nourishing music. These events have become so rare in our lives that we have lost the ability to even recognize what will nourish us. It may seem basic, and almost trivial, to even mention these actions, but most of us do not indulge anymore in these great instances of life. I invite you to take time for yourself. It will replenish what the days' frenzy takes away.

Love for ourselves is one of the basic ingredients in the recipe for a balanced life, it is a regenerating tank where the production of love for others and the appreciation for our own existence happen. Since we give what we have let's respect ourselves, our body, our mind, and our spirit acknowledging the "whole self" and take care of it so that we will be able to pour it onto others. Having these aforementioned moments of self-appreciation will allow us to re-establish and reclaim a relationship with ourselves.

How frequently we find ourselves blaming others for taking too much of our time or asking too much of us, and we may blame ourselves for giving undeserved attention, care, or time to others. Reality is that we might have given them everything to the point of bankrupting our own reservoir because the thought of replenishing what was being depleted has not yet come to mind. There may no longer be any fuel left to function, but we keep on going until our engine *demands* us stop, causing us to reach the point of breaking down.

Missing opportunities to regenerate will end up leaving us with an empty and dry reservoir, nothing left to give, nothing left to love, no light, no shine attracting other's love towards us. To complicate things, often when we deny self-love moments we may end up blaming others for our isolation and depletion, without realizing that *we* stopped loving ourselves in the first place. Carve "Me" moments into your life and respect them as sacred love for yourselves, re-instate or establish daily "Me" moments with all the available technology disconnected, cherish those few minutes of silence where we do nothing but listen to that silence, tune in with it, and do nothing. Just "be." Ultimately, you have to teach yourself to "be" rather than to "do."

In following this daily practice, you will learn the following:

> How to be in the present moment—not just glancing at your surroundings, but finally noticing the perfection around you, without needing to add anything.

Just one moment of silence may be enough to help you to go much deeper into yourself and to remain connected with your true Self.

Being content with what you see and what you are able to touch can help you with not needing to have something different or simply something more, in order to be satisfied.

Our heart is always talking to us, but our mind, and our ego, has a much louder voice. If we do not turn the volume of our mind down, we cannot listen to our inner Self. We keep living blindly, trying to follow paths that, most of the time, are not the right ones for us. Realization of this comes too late when the disappointment and pain have already caught up with us, and when the consequences are bigger than we expected them to be.

Cherish and make those moments an inescapable daily ritual so that you take care of the non-material part of you through them, you will learn to meet, to listen and to become acquainted with your inner Self and keep your connection with the Source. It will transform the practical part of your life which will then start to reveal itself with less or no trauma, pain, fear, or anxiety, because you will be finally able to follow your inner guidance and irrevocably, hear your heart.

Accept to take all the love you have around you and allow yourself to see it. It will fill up the gap—the void you might feel at times when the unwanted happens. When we must hold the pain of that unwanted and undesirable occurrence, this is the exact time we need to nourish ourselves with love.

Love is intertwined with *forgiveness*. If we cannot pour love out indiscriminately on everybody, how can we learn forgiveness and vice versa, how can we forgive if we do not love?

CHAPTER 3

STEP TWO: FORGIVENESS

> *"Forgiveness is the fragrance that the violet sheds on the heel that has crushed it.[3]"*
>
> — *Mark Twain*

Forgiveness is another practice not easy to master, but is essential in order to grow up. As Mark Twain said it in the most beautiful way, forgiveness is the response we decide to have to an unkind, wounding act and it is not directly proportional to the deed of hurt we have received. Forgiveness has nothing to do with condoning or excusing hurtful actions, this is absolutely untrue and is something which should remain clear. Therefore, it is necessary to emphasize two facts:

Firstly, forgiving is each individual's own private and most intimate business that must happen within yourself, it is about letting go of the heavy load we are carrying as a consequence of hurtful deeds towards us, whether they be real or perceived. Dragging that pain and heaviness into and throughout our life will only serve one purpose: to hurt and damage us more than any pain inflicted on us could have ever done by itself.

Secondly, forgiving neither means condoning nor excusing or justifying the doing of whom has betrayed our love and trust or even abused us. Forgiving does not mean to forgive and then continue to expose ourselves to the "abuser" or "breacher of trust" either. Forgiving means *genuinely* no longer feeling resentful in our hearts and wishing well to those who have hurt us—even if these good wishes can be sent from afar.

Conversely, if we are unable to forgive, we chain ourselves to our perpetrators, whether we are physically close to them or not. Moreover, we will be giving them power over us, forcing us to live with their poison, its toxicity (and all the side effects that come with it) twenty-four hours a day. And what does that do to the perpetrators? *N o t h i n g*. And what does it do to us? It will affect our lives enormously. Moments of joy will be missed or shadowed and eclipsed by the negativity and toxicity of our anger, resentment, frustration and pain. Forgiving, instead, has a great positive impact and power on the quality of our own life—on our daily outcome.

The wisdom of the teachings of Thich Nhat Hanh, which I have read thousands of times and I continue to read, has particularly helped in moments when I found myself stuck in negative emotions and could not move further into forgiveness. Thich Nhat Hanh says that when we are hurt by someone, it is because their heart is not able to contain the suffering they experience and it leaks out, affecting other people. The worst we can do is punish them, because what they really need is forgiveness and support. When we suffer at the hands of somebody else we do not care about giving them our support, right? The fact of the matter is that there is nothing we can do to relieve our suffering unless we are willing to forgive. It is the *only* way to relieve our suffering. None of us can endure the load of anger and resentment without being consumed, drained, and emptied.

Many times—too often—I hear someone describing the wounds they have acquired and suffered by others. They become almost aggressive when I try to steer the conversation back to them, away from those people who hurt them. I hear, "You do not understand how... what *he/she* has done to me." Or: "Yes I understand *but they/he/she...*" I notice that there is almost always a need to explain more about the event that caused them pain, and about the people involved to justify the unwillingness to forgive. These are unnecessary responses to cover up our *resistance* to forgive.

There is no need whatsoever to go through the path of re-calling and re-experiencing the painful occurrence and those who hurt us, whether they are guilty of the offense or not. Forgiving is our own business, and it does take place in the most intimate space of ourselves: our heart. Forgiveness happens in the seclusion of our heart. Be assured that your heart will then soften, your soul will rejoice, and your life will expand. You will feel *more*. You will be free to experience the details of your existence. The sun will shine more and it will warm you more, the smiles given to you will mean more, the flowers you see will be more of a miracle to you, all because you removed your resistance to forgive, and instead you allowed it. Only now, is there room for joy and peace.

Somewhere, as a teenager, I heard that we are victims when we allow somebody to be our executioner. That's when I realized that there is always a choice to make. At these crossroads, we can choose the victim's path or the victorious path. We need to realize that choosing the path of the victim is like living a life with no bliss, joy, humor, love, compassion, and all those ingredients that make a life worth living. It is instead, like living a lifeless life, a life where the vital signs of it are reduced to the negative until it reaches the unavoidable sad end of it. The victorious pathway will allow our life to expand and joy to enter every possible aspect of our lives. We will be able to live in the moment—with all its special manifestations and facets, really living and not just killing time. Let's consider this: don't we want to make sure that when this earthly journey is over we have truly *lived*?

Forgiveness, like love, is a step that must start with ourselves; forgiving ourselves is crucial to start our healing process. We must remove any senses of guilt we might have and simply express love, respect, *and* forgiveness to ourselves. Only then can we apply the same forgiveness to others, reminding ourselves that we are not taking away the person's responsibility for that action, nor condoning their behavior or reestablishing a connection we might have had with that or those individuals. We must keep in mind that in this life we are given a certain amount of time available and, as we cannot overload our day with an excessive number of tasks, we cannot load our lives with tasks that won't bring us any good like carrying resentment and anger therefore wasting the precious time gifted to us.

The wiser choice is to use our time to keep the focus on our intentions, on the outcome we want for this dance we call life. When we lose our focus because of frustration or pain caused by others, we need to ask ourselves, "Do I follow and react to this new path that has presented itself to me, or do I keep my focus on my original intention?" Is my true life's purpose to *show* the world *I am right?* Or is it to focus on my purpose and intention and rather *get it right?* It is better and most sensible to keep our focus on our intention and life purpose since intention is the powerful energy that changes our lives. Thus: love, forgive, and bless. I do understand that this can be very difficult to accomplish when we are suffering for what we feel others did or do to us.

Once we acquire the ability to forgive, the engine is moving again towards life. We learn to live a present that will create a solid, positive past for our future. Conversely, if we do not ascertain how to forgive, we remain frozen in the past with all event or occurrence that we so much wish to forget. All the opportunities to leap into our future will be locked up. Present and future will be the same as our past, and our future will have the same past we have now—the same one that we wish so much to erase.

One of my recommendations is to be very careful to not mislead yourself since we can be the best deceiver of ourselves. It's not enough to say, "I forgive him/her," and when somebody mentions the person who we hold anger for, our blood rushes and pulses faster through our veins. We need to mean it, we need to really own that forgiveness and release that burden preventing us from moving forward. One more thing to bear in mind, which is necessary to emphasize, is that before reaching true forgiveness, we need to go through and familiarize ourselves with the pain and the hurt emanating from the wound which we carry. Only after experiencing that pain do we put the healing process in motion, therefore we must not despair if we cannot forgive right away, we need to give ourselves the gift to wish to forgive and the healing process will run its course.

Forgiveness is also the direct link to compassion. If forgiveness is not reached, gaining compassion for those who have hurt us is not possible. Not only that, but compassion on a larger scale cannot be known, it cannot be met, lived or experienced. As all of these seven steps described in these pages, compassion must start toward ourselves, by not forgiving we would be sadly incapable of being compassionate towards ourselves and others giving birth to dynamics that will widen the distance more and more between us and the potential joy and peace in our lives.

CHAPTER 4

STEP THREE: COMPASSION

"Compassion happens when we see, hear, and feel beyond ourselves."

— *Antonella Lo Re*

Compassion is the inner ability to expand and extend our empathy towards others. It is some kind of feeling we experience for another person's pain, trouble or affliction, not to be confused with the feeling of pity or sorrow, but rather a profound understanding of their situation. Compassion is a feeling that should motivate us into action, even if that action is simply stopping ourselves from judging, from attempting to provide our solution but limiting ourselves and instead offering a listening ear. Listening is key and it is the only path to achieve true compassion. A few words are necessary on *listening* here because nowadays it seems to be a daunting task for everybody. We run, we touch everything and everybody on the surface, we hear everything, but we listen to nothing, so little time to stop and listen. We certainly are no longer able to listen to each other's voices, occasionally we pretend to listen while our mind spaces out on its own errands. What greater value is there than that which comes with feeling heard when we talk to somebody? Regrettably, we are unable to even listen to ourselves and to what we should listen to most: our inner voice. Our inner voice is always whispering—listen, without adding anything.

Nothing is more important than being heard. In fact, when we feel listened to in times of hardship, we feel a sense of relief, as if sharing our pain has lightened the burden we are carrying on our shoulders. Feeling heard enables us to quiet down our own pains and worries even if only for a short while. We should really put everything else on "pause" and go back to listening as the prioritized task of our daily life.

In Italian, there is only one verb that translates into the English "hear and feel": *Sentire*. It specifically means "receiving an impression through the senses"—hearing being one of the senses. Compassion is the ability to *Sentire,* to feel the depth of another's pain. Even if only for a short fragment of time, if it touches something deep inside of us, we are able to truly feel it. All we have to do is feel it and offer an active, listening ear. It is right through active listening that the heart is engaged and open, thus there is no gap between our capacity to feel and someone else's pain. It may be only for few seconds, but in that time, our souls are so close that we can feel through our senses what the other person, in his/her deep emotions, is experiencing.

One of my most valuable lessons in comprehending compassion has been learning that being compassionate does not mean having to offer a solution. Most often, it means to listen with an open heart, period. Instead we tend to offer judgements coming from an endless flow of omniscience. We often hear omniscient assumptions of someone's tough and challenging situation and plenty of judgement for that person's action or behavior, we get to *know* how they feel why they feel, how they should feel instead and what the source of their trouble is.

In truth, though, when dealing with someone else's trouble, not having answers—especially the ones we fabricate—can be a very good thing, a true blessing for them and for ourselves. In fact, showing true compassion, however, should compel us to refrain from performing this cheap analysis. As soon as we start our omniscient report, we should stop and ask ourselves, "Do I *really* and *truly* know the why, what, and how of this person's actions and behavior? Do I really know what makes them act this way? What keeps them awake at night? What makes them cry?" We should stop there before beginning our report of conjectures, allegations, and speculations.

Refraining from constructing an omniscient report will make us feel more openhearted toward the world. This includes people we love, those we do not like, people we meet only occasionally, and those we have not chosen in our life but cannot fire or in any way divorce—usually family members or relatives. Just stop and think of what they might be going through and what has influenced them to act a certain way. Step into their skin for a moment and feel their pain. That's it. If you perceive a lack of love, send them love. If you perceive pain, send them joy.

I found it very helpful when I heard Deepak Chopra saying that by judging, a turbulence is created that blocks us from connecting with the Higher Self. Relinquishing the need to judge others enables us to reach that place of deep stillness. We should remind ourselves, "Today I will judge nobody" every day. Using it as a mantra, and try to do our best with it. There will be good and bad days, but on the best ones, we will feel a deeper connection to the Source of the Universe. I experienced myself that in my best days the inclination of the ground I was walking on was much less steep, life was less blurry, and I felt more welcomed, more loved, and more connected to all the good that life was gifting me with. I hope you'll want to give it a try so that you will be able to feel a sense of relief that will wash over you once you realize how that judging was weighing on you. You will feel freer and more lighthearted.

All that is really needed to reach true compassion is listening with an open heart, without judging and without offering solutions, because sometimes there are *no* solutions.

As with the other seven steps, before practicing with others, it is important to learn how to be merciful and compassionate with yourself first. The love and forgiveness you will experience internally will allow you to offer it to others. Be compassionate to yourself and just start treat yourself as if you are the person you love most every single moment of your days. You will then be able to radiate that energy out and pour it onto others.

Compassion toward ourselves will help us reconnect with the Self, rather than continue identifying with our perpetrators or betrayers. We need to bear in mind that it is within us, we do not have to seek compassion like we do not have to seek love, it is within us. Listen to others' pain and be compassionate, you will receive it too. You will be heard, and you will be grateful for being listened to.

CHAPTER 5

STEP FOUR: GRATITUDE

"Gratitude is the beam of light you give back once you have acknowledged the bright light shining on you."

— *Antonella Lo Re*

I consider gratitude the fuel of our wonders. Gratitude is an act of kindness in itself but also a way to ask for more of what we are grateful of since the Universe responds to our gratitude by showering us with more of what our heart rejoices for. Meister Eckhart said, "If the only prayer you ever say in your entire life is thank you, that will be enough."[4]

As human beings, we are always so absorbed taking from everything and everyone that we have little time for even the smallest gesture of gratitude, either out in the street or within our family. Wouldn't it be beautiful if, at the end of our day, we collected our thoughts and gave thanks for the day?

When my daughter was a toddler, I started a new habit called "laugh therapy." Just before going to bed, I made sure to watch something on television that made me laugh out loud at the same time I started a "thanks–giving" practice every night with my "thank you book," as I called it.

Every night I took the time to laugh and write in my journal. It was a log of what I was grateful for that day, even if only the laugh I had at the comedy show, I soon found out that I could recall more and more positivity that had happened in my day. The longer I thought about my day the more gratitude I would discover.

It has been a fantastic exercise, my little one used to say it was a *splendastic* exercise, to recall the little moments of kindness I gave and received each day. My pages were soon full of events to be thankful for. A short while after this practice I noticed that focusing on what I was grateful for helped the day's disappointments and blocks to melt away, diluted the pain, and highlighted the good things, even if only little. A sense of joy surrounded me and grew throughout the week. My gratitude included:

Thank you for the neighbor's "Good morning!"

Thank you for the smile and tighter-than-yesterday hug my baby gave me.

Thank you for the flower blooming from my orchid.

Gratitude for these seemingly minor events can really help us store the goodness of our days in our mind. Before, they had simply melted away, overpowered, overshadowed, and often wiped out by the only bad thing that happened that day, like an unexpected bill, the plumber who needed to be called twice before repairing the furnace, or even more serious issues, like worrying about financial issues, a career, and about the future.

I highly recommend writing down what we are thankful for at night time after the occurrences throughout our day, this will prevent the one bad or negative event of that day from dominating the little positive things. Gratitude is a constructive way to end your day, and it's a very little exercise that amounts to huge benefits besides helping to sleep better with a more serene and lighter heart.

This exercise helps us to be more aware of our surroundings, we notice things that have been unnoticed forever like the chirping of the birds, a sunrise, and a sunset. We end up being thankful and encouraged to enjoy for being able to see them, feel them, and hear them. Rereading the entries of our journal at the end of the week can really brighten up our life. We end up by being consciously focused on the half-full glass before we ever notice the empty part. We experience a new way of living and a new opening that will make us rewrite our life tale in a complete new light and fashion.

Being deliberately grateful is a ritual that we all should embrace and practice because being grateful has a domino effect on our life. We become more positive, more open to receiving and giving, with a greater balance for both. As we express more gratitude for the positive things in our life, more good flows our way. I experienced as if an unlimited Source was pouring onto me the blessings and magnificence I had overlooked for many years. What I received in return was more than I could wrap my head around.

In practicing conscious gratitude, I have learned that magic unity of two powerful forces: Giving and Receiving. Life is orchestrated by the rhythm of giving and receiving. Most of us may have been raised being taught that giving is important. It is what makes us good friends, good neighbors, good Christians, good children of God, good sons and daughters, good girls… The teaching of receiving, however, has been somewhat neglected. The art of receiving is as equally important as the art of giving. It's part of one Unity. Gibran, in *The Prophet*[5], speaks about joy and sorrow being part of the same circle, unit, or Unity. For our experience to be complete, we must encounter and accept both sides; in this case, receiving as well as giving. Knowing how to give is learning to give just for the sake of the act. No payback, expectations, recognition, or rewards are involved in "giving."

The art of receiving implies being grateful for whatever we receive, or simply appreciating the gesture of giving. A smile, a flower, an acknowledgement, a costly or inexpensive gift—the material or immaterial benefit does *not* change the value of the intent of giving. Receiving with an open heart and gratitude for the value of the gesture is what counts.

If pure gratitude is not there, we become "takers," not "receivers." If we take and do not learn how to receive, we will soon forget the value of what we were offered. The emptiness and the need for more, and the need of filling up that bottomless container that will never be full, regardless of how much we take, will stay with us. Takers never remember what was given to them. Somebody can list for them what life has provided, but they will not remember. If we do allow and learn how to receive with true gratitude everything will be locked in the compartment of all things forgotten, and we become oblivious of the treasures and gifts we have received. Most likely, we are only able to take note of what was *not* given to us.

Be a great giver as much as a great receiver. Start by saying "thank you" for a compliment, or if we are told we are good at something. Accept it. Open your heart and make it sound the note of gratitude, saying a heartfelt "thank you." Whatever "bad" things you may have done, you are a Divine creature. If somebody recognizes that, they saw the Divine traits in you. Do the same for others. Genuinely open your heart and give them a caress of kindness, recognizing their Divine greatness.

Pour love, acts of kindness and gratitude out around you and you will be surrounded by it. Do not be concerned about whom you are giving love and kindness to. Whoever they are, it's none of our business to judge and determine if they deserve it or not. That is between the Universe and them. Simply be thankful, and more of what you are thankful for will manifest for you.

Mother Teresa is credited with saying that she alone could not change the world, but she could cast a stone across the waters, therefore creating many ripples. Even if we cannot change the world with a single action, we can always start there and see the positive effects it creates.

CHAPTER 6

STEP FIVE: ACCEPTANCE

"Acceptance is the understanding of the useless and futile effort of swimming upstream."

— *Antonella Lo Re*

In reading Eckhart Tolle's book, *The Power of Now: A Guide to Spiritual Enlightenment*,[6] I discerned it is crucial to accept the moment as it is and become fully acquainted with it. Accept what the present moment offers and work with it as if we have handpicked it. Doing so will change our entire life. Upon first reading the message, however, my physical body expressed an immediate resistance. It reacted strongly, not accepting it. I thought, "How can this be possible? He does not know what we are really talking about here. How can he suggest accepting and enduring something which is clearly not what I have chosen?" At that time, I was facing a harsh moment that I *insisted* I could not have chosen. Today it must be admitted that acceptance together with forgiveness was probably the most difficult lesson for me to learn. I have had to work on this issue harder than anything else, and it is, or I am, still a work in progress.

Each of the seven inner abilities (Love, Forgiveness, Compassion, Gratitude, Acceptance, Silence, and Trust) has taken me a long time to process and make my own. When I first began looking for this spiritual thread I had lost, I understood the abilities intellectually, but they were not part of me, they were not fully digested and absorbed, therefore not owned by me. It was a long time before assimilation was complete, and even now, I still need to work on maintaining the seven abilities, I have good and not-so-good days.

Do you recall finding yourself in the most difficult time of your life as you can remember, when you fought and questioned. "Why?" It is right when anger builds up; we shout about the unfairness we are suffering from, at times we rage our fury. We shout loud "Why has this happened to me?" We insistently repeat in resistance "NO!" We object to the giant in front of us unfortunately only to see it growing bigger and bigger. I went through that.

My body and my heart, could no longer contain any additional moves of life's brutal game. I wanted the world to recognize the cruelty being done to me. How dare the world not stop and do something about that injustice, that in-humaneness? Why was the world so merciless? I yelled at the Universe with rage, communicated my rage to people, shouting out, "Why do you people do not see? Why don't you comprehend? How can you, God, allow this to happen?"

What a long exercise, trial and error, tears and anger before understanding that the wisest and more beneficial way to go is non-resistance, therefore acceptance. To make it mine more than intellectually took a long time and still, if some of you wonders, I do get mad, I do resist, I do dislike but to get to the point of wondering: what for? After my reading of Eckhart Tolle, I began to understand that if we learn how to surrender, we transform our resistance into acceptance consequently becoming able to find the long-sought-after "peace." Peace. That *is* the magic word—all we long for.

Revenge, showing the world we are right, exposing the meanness inherent in what we suffer, would not get us there. Peace is what we most want—and need. Our fits, our tantrums, our rage against the difficult time we are going through is not taking or moving us anywhere, instead, it just freezes us in that terrible moment making it eternal.

However, when we create resistance to what's happening we give away our power and most of the time we transfer that power to our perpetrators or anyway to the cause of our suffering. This is the right moment when we must comprehend that it is time to no longer give power to anyone, allowing them to become our perpetrator and take back our power. Tough work, but worth it. When life is difficult, when fears are overwhelming, when the future is a humongous monster we believe we cannot face we must turn to surrender. We must begin by accepting every single day, every single step of the day, and focusing on the present. That is all we might have on our side: the present moment.

I feel that what I am writing and trying to convey in this next paragraph is true and accurate. I felt it, I experienced it, I lived it, and it did really work.

When facing an unexpected and shocking situation, before you take any deliberate action against it, pause. Put your automatic, visceral reaction aside and do *no-thing*. Do not label it. Do not define it. Do not classify it as good or bad. Just allow it. Observe it passing by before you. Allow the moment to be *as it is*. Do not try to understand, just quiet down your mind. The resistance you immediately and automatically react with will make you even more miserable. Understand this, it may sound very difficult to do, but it is *so* necessary. Allow the moment to be as it is. Whatever it is, that's enough. I am not suggesting you be happy about it, or enjoy it. Just allow it, with no resistance. Let it go by.

If you stop it in order to fight it, it will be much more painful. It can become excruciating. Surrender. Learn to surrender. Every step leads somewhere. Even what you do not want to happen—as painful as it may be—is a stepping stone leading you where you need to go.

As far as I am concerned, practicing this has been another time-consuming transformation; it has taken years of work to achieve a measure of success. If you can, understand this now while you are reading it and make it yours. Whatever you have to face, accept it and surrender to it. Do not allow your mind to create fiction and wander around it, or try to understand it. Become acquainted with not knowing, that is fine. It's the greatest favor you can give yourself.

Conversely, if you refuse to accept the situation and surrender to it you risk losing yourself in the pages of your "good reason to be a victim" book. As we are the best deceivers of ourselves, we can easily turn onto the mischievous path of reasons why this bad thing has happened to us and end up losing track of what really happened to us versus what we feel happened to us—the reality versus the emotions.

For instance, if you receive the shocking news of being laid off, it's almost automatic to respond with a common sort of resistance that is hardly ever really thought out or intended, like, "A door is closing and a better one will open for me." Instead of wasting time having an emotional tantrum over what has just happened, you need to train yourself to be open to what might happen and prepare yourself for that new beginning. Surrender and accept. What will happen is in the hand of the Universe.

It is right when the unwanted happens that we must learn to hold the pain. Yes, pain and suffering are sometimes unavoidable, but once you understand you are able to hold that pain, you will see that right there lies your opportunity, that suffering will become a light you never could have imagined. Processing pain and sorrow this way will transform you, it will teach you so much and it will propel you forward in your evolution. Even amidst the most painful afflictions, betrayals, and unexpected shocks, remind yourself to stay focused on what matters: the present moment.

All occurrences in life shall pass and the essence of life will be still with us. This one more experience will have moved us forward as long as we accept it. Acceptance is what roots us in the present moment and makes us transform the negative into positive. Whatever we believe we have to resist and not accept is what will lead us to new opportunities.

CHAPTER 7

STEP SIX: SILENCE

> *"Listening is the prelude to peace."*
>
> — *Antonella Lo Re*

Working on yourself is a choice, and sometimes it is not as easy as it seems. It takes courage to admit that we do not know something, and it's even more confusing and disorienting when we realize that we do not know what is that we don't know. Often in our search for our spiritual thread, at first, we need to search so much that we are randomly moving outside ourselves. We read, we research, we attend workshops of all kinds, hoping they can satisfy the endless thirst and need for answers.

I have myself gone through that, and found that all of these attempts brought something new into my life, and they were necessary learning experiences. I recall talking to all sorts of people with the most diverse experiences and life stories I could find. Eventually, though, I reached the absolute conviction that what I really needed was within me. I needed to get in touch with that inner Self somehow. I realized that I needed to work on whatever resistance I found within and I had to go deeper and deeper. Now my searching was focused and I had defined a meaningful task. I was searching for something that could teach me how to go deeper inside myself.

An old man, a wonderful soul in my life, once told me a story that I remember this way:

Angels were called up to a meeting to decide where to put *all* the answers for Man to tap into that were necessary for him to face life and gain wisdom. They all gathered together and, one by one, each suggested a location.

"We should put all the answers in the deepest ocean," said one.

All the other angels in a chorus replied, "No, it would be too hard for Man to find them."

Another angel suggested, "Let's put them on the very top of the highest mountain!!!"

The chorus resonated, saying, "Yes!"

But another angel spoke up. "No, Man will be too tired when he finds them."

After many attempts to find the best location for wisdom, a little angel came up with an idea. "Let's put *all* the answers within Man…inside him."

I found the story very unusual at the time, but it made me think that somehow, I needed to reach deeper inside myself and explore, trying to find the answers I needed. But how was I supposed to reach so far within? Silence has been my answer. Silence was the way.

Learning more with my Buddhist acquaintance but having, at the time, sporadic time available for practice, I had only given meditation a short try. I decided to set more time aside. Little by little, an entirely new Universe opened up for me! But let me tell you my experience with meditation and silence.

Silence? For me, it was not easy, as this is not a naturally occurring trait of my personality. When I first tried meditation, it was extremely difficult to quiet my mind. I would sit in a so-called "comfortable position," as the instructor would suggest, but I was never comfortable. Not even close to being comfortable. Then, I started to acquaint myself with my body, especially with my desire to look, appear, or perform in the best way possible. I understood it was not a competition with myself—or with anyone else—and it had even less than nothing to do with my ability to "perform." It became clear to me that when St. Francis de Sales said, "What we need is a cup of understanding, a barrel of love, and an ocean of patience," he must have been talking about meditation.

After many attempts, I could finally sit still—in as comfortable of a position I could get myself into. I took deep breath after deep breath, again following the instructions and trying hard to concentrate on my breathing. Unrequested and unwanted thoughts would pop up. If I had just one lovely second of relaxation, I automatically thought, "This would be so good for my daughter, Emma…" Or that "I really needed to read this or that", "talk to such-and-such", "go to these places", "run those errands", so on and so forth …while all I had worked so hard on would fade away. Does anybody relates to this provocative thought flow?

We do need to slowly learn to accept those thoughts without judging them as wanted or unwanted, as nasty or pleasant thoughts, we must just accept and allowing them as an unavoidable part of our experience. We must let these thoughts be and return to our breathing, focusing on our breathing. Accepting those "distractions" and instead almost welcoming them gives us the total experience of the moment without resistance.

Some of you might relate to physical sensations, all those kinds of itches that we suddenly noticed, or even pain. Why do these things pop up now? Why now, while we are so determined to try to relax, feel at ease, and "meditate"? It is because we must learn to allow these thoughts so that they pass through instead of holding a place in our minds. Our mind wanders and wanders, and all we need is to learn to notice it wandering and accept it. Meditation or a moment of silence and relaxation are absolutely a must-do practice everyday. The reason why I also refer to meditation as silence is because I know how many of us are intimidated by the word meditation. As a matter of fact, many people tell me that meditation is very difficult for them and they won't give it a try. But starting with simple relaxation in silence is a huge step towards re-connecting with our inner Self. We need to form a new intention to give ourselves a few minutes of silence every day. It is important though to remember why we made the pledge in the first place so that, for example when our subconscious suggests us to *"skip it for today"* we pause and anyway go to that little corner we have carved for ourselves and start our new experience of silence.

At first we might not always accomplish it—having good days and bad days— but it is important is to return to it as soon as possible and make silence part of our lifestyle. Then, without realizing it, the silence will last longer and longer until we find ourselves practicing probably thirty minutes every day, and sometimes multiple times a day. I, personally, am still working on the ocean of patience.

You will find out that those moments of silence give you the realization of the here and now, the right moment. What you are doing, what you are seeing, what you are touching in this right moment is what you can enjoy deeply and truly. There are no more fears for what might happen tomorrow: whether you do not get paid or if you cannot find another contract or if you get fired; no more doubts about something that might be happening. No more fears for something that may never even happen. Right now is what counts.

Right now, while I am here trying to put my thoughts into words and seeing words and phrases appear before my eyes gives me the joy and happiness of a child in front of a magic dream being unveiled. I remember how many sunsets used to pass unnoticed, how many flowers used to pass unnoticed. Now I stop, I notice, I breathe them in, and I share them. This is what the transformation of mindfulness and awareness has given me and can give you too. A day is made up of little moments. If we learn how to live each moment deeply and enjoy it, our day is transformed. Every day try to remind yourself to stop running and chasing whatever goal or target you have for that day, for that week, for that month, or for that year. If we do not learn to stop and be silent, that objective will only keep on moving, going further and further away from us while our life flies by.

I will never stress the importance of the present moment enough. We all tend to postpone peace and happiness. While complaining for our stress and sadness we say, "*This* is why I am not happy, but when I get this or that…" whatever *this* might be: a new house… a new job… going on vacation… "when, when, when…" the *when* becomes the moment of our happiness while we forget that the future is an illusion not a certainty. We are so good at filling our minds up with so many wishes that we end up wishing our life away. If we give ourselves the gift of solitude and silence, and honor it, we understand it is an inexhaustible source of nourishment that will give us the essential nutrients we need to embark on and navigate our life voyage, and to dance at the rhythm of its music. We must make the effort to live in the moment and to breath the present moment. Noticing our surroundings and touching what is here in front of us. With this practice, everything becomes easier and more bearable even in challenging times.

Through an acquainted silence, we will get to know our sense of Self, we will get to know our needs, fears, limits, and hopes. We will acquire love for ourselves therefore learn to give love to others. We will respect ourselves and we will be able to respect others; we will learn how to be honest with ourselves so we can be to others; we will learn how to be compassionate with ourselves so we will feel compassion for others.

In addition, while meditation and silence is finding a space to listen within and listen to the Divine voice, prayer is our way to talk to the Divine. Both listening and praying are the two ways necessary to keep this marvelous dialogue going. My wish to you: Be mindful of what is going on in the moment. Have your moment of silence, and listen.

CHAPTER 8

STEP SEVEN: TRUST

"Faith is the certainty that everything is taken care of for you."

— *Antonella Lo Re*

For the seventh step, I will address faith and trust. You will see I use the two interchangeably and the reason I refer to faith as "trust" is because I do not refer to religious faith. Many people are not religious but still have a strong faith. I want to speak about faith and trust in a Divine Source, trust in something *greater* than us whether it derives from an organized religion we belong to or whether it is a natural occurrence and we have no particular, pre-established beliefs.

There are those who claim they don't have faith in anything. But in fact, you can see that they do. They may not believe in organized religion, but we all have a strong *trust* in something. Unfortunately, it seems that our faith and trust in the negative grows and we begin to believe in that so vigorously. We hear faith in the negative so often: "I am sure that [the unwanted thing] is going to happen," "I am sure I won't be able to make it," "I am sure this illness will be so devastating that I will not recover." This is *amazing* faith however we use it incorrectly, we are often confident that the negative things will certainly happen and do not have faith in the positive. Less frequently do we hear the other, side: "I am sure this illness will not last," "I am sure my recovery will be shorter than foreseen," "I am sure I will find a job." We must practice our doubtless trust in what is positive and possible, even if we do not see it. We need to be more like the flower that starts growing between the concrete, it never doubts whether it will be a flower or not, it simply grows.

We should remind ourselves of the existence of two planes: physical and spiritual. Neither of them denies the other. In our three-dimensional physical reality, there are many limits that we constantly trust and draw from—space, time, and opportunities. Conversely, in the spiritual realm, there are no such restrictions, but there are rather infinite possibilities and potentials we can trigger and prompt through our intentions. Faith means letting go of the physical (a confined and limited realm) and stepping into the spiritual, a limitless one. We must let the Universe work relinquishing any wish, control, or desire on our part.

Faith works as an antidote to our fears. Think for a moment whenever we need to face the unknown, only faith can help us to go ahead and embrace it. Once we relinquish our control and let trust come in fears subside, doubts cannot survive, and anxieties and worries vanish, leaving us with an immense, invaluable peace, no matter what. When we have true faith we are feeling taken care of. Faith, can be like reaching out and touching the hand of the Source, His hand, and feeling an exchange, reciprocation and a wonderful sense of acknowledgement.

Nevertheless, sometimes we wonder how to conquer faith and how to keep it. One day I heard a spiritual teacher answering the question, "How can I keep my faith?" He replied with another question: "How do you keep yourself fit and your muscles toned? Practice, practice, practice." As per my experience, faith is a continuous workout. As we exercise our muscles by going to the gym, we should exercise the "muscles" of our spirituality by continuing to build faith and trust in the Universe. As we keep our brain alert by reading and studying, we should do the same with the spiritual part of ourselves. We need to train and work out the spiritual part in us before it forgets what being "toned" means. Someone once said, "Practice shapes you beyond your will." When I heard that, it woke me up. I started that practice, that exercise, that shapes me beyond my will.

One day a seven year old girl, sat me down and explained that one of her classmates confided that he did not believe in Santa. She was shocked and nearly devastated. But after giving me such horrific news, she sweetly consoled herself, and also me, by saying, "Well, there are many people who unfortunately do not believe in God. That is sad because He is. It is not a question of believing or not, *He is*!" I saw the *faith* in this little girl—her doubtless trust in what "*is,*" as she said.

Children have a wonderful trust in the unknown. Dig into your heart and rediscover the trust that is in you. Trust and faith will resurface and build up through perseverance, patience, and practice. Practice, practice, and practice.

Religion or Spirituality?

In the world of spiritual growth and personal development, seekers are those who take a path of self-discovery in their life. It is key to search for your connection to the Higher Source in life. You will discover what your own unique purpose is, fulfill it, thereby evolving.

Spirituality and religion do not necessarily have to converge. Sometimes they do, and other times they do not. There are people who live a great spiritual life without closeness to any organized religion. At times, very religious people do not have spirituality—the close connection to the Source.

Religion is a suggested path to follow in order to connect with God more closely. Spirituality is your own private path to connect to God, the Higher Source, the Universe, the Energy of all creation, or to whatever name you are giving to it. Everybody who embarks upon a spiritual path calls it by a different name. Spirituality is your own experience of connection with the Higher Source, whatever your journey toward that might be. Religion or Spirituality?

CHAPTER 9

THE PATH TO JOY

Life is made of both suffering *and* bliss. There is no way to avoid suffering but if we adopt these seven steps it will be easier to face the unwanted while keeping a state of peace. Every one of us has a painful story, right? For some reason, pain never misses its target—it has not missed any of us in one way or another and it is part of the rhythm of life, with its ups and downs. What is important is to ask ourselves, "Can I use my pain, can my painful experience serve me to grow and evolve?" Whenever you have a challenge in front of you, you also have the power within yourself to face it.

It is often said that any painful experience or sorrow is an opportunity. On one hand suffering helps us to refine compassion towards ourselves and towards others. When we live through personal hardship, we can learn to step inside someone's skin and deeply understand another's afflictions. Suffering softens our heart and polishes our ability to be compassionate. On the other hand, bliss and joy, inspire and motivate us and drive us to move forward in the best possible way.

Life manifests itself in this duality every day; joy and affliction, giving and receiving, success and failure, life and death. We created an illusion that life is what we our ego wants to see, but reality is that life is part of a unity with its opposites. Both sides will share their uniqueness with us and will teach us to evolve and grow, this is the very reason why we should learn acceptance and not discard any of these opposites to fully experience our earthly journey. If we think about success, for example, don't we know that before a success, there is always at least one failure? We must learn how to fail. Accept, and fail *well*. Let's learn to embrace the pain of that failure, the disappointment, and ask ourselves, "What do I need to learn from this?" To live fully means to go through the pain of the failure and the bliss of the success, the only way to achieve and fulfill our own purpose in life.

We always need to remember that it is through all the constrictions in life, those tiring and difficult passages into the narrowest, darkest, and inescapable tunnel of life, we are introduced to our true Self, and also to our gifts, to our strengths and our power. Whenever we stumble, whenever we fall, we are only experiencing life. That is the truthful meaning of our journey. No matter the events, look up, look forward. Any experience in life should not go to waste but rather be a path thorough which our soul and spirit grow, progress and evolve. The more you are open to accept our pain or our limitations, the more we are connected with our inner Self.

When having our so-called "bad days," acceptance is what should be practiced first, when we need to reach for a thought that feels better in the attempt to tune ourselves towards the positive. Acceptance is one of the hardest steps, it needs a lot of work but strongly encourage you to do it, it pays off. When we resist, life becomes uselessly harder. Life is like music, we need to dance and move to its rhythm. The moment we do not accept the rhythm and resist, we clash, and everything becomes awkwardly difficult. When we follow the rhythm, we may not know what is next, yet we are not afraid of what is to come. We let our bodies flow until the music ends. The rhythm may change constantly, but all we need to do is continue dancing fearlessly and trusting that everything will be all right. Trust is another inner ability we must refine in order to make ours the fact that we are not alone and we are always taken care of.

When Emotions Arise

Emotions are our pitfalls. Unfortunately, we are not taught how to deal with rising and overwhelming emotions. We either fall into a defensive mode, or work hard to suppress them. These actions give birth to a seed that soon becomes a giant sequoia, and a heavy burden that will haunt us forever. We cannot deny the emotions that arise from an abusive situation, a failure, a betrayal, a bad day, disrespect, disappointment, or grief. We need to learn how to observe our emotions, even negative ones. Accept them, recognize them, observe them and most of all do not suppress them, accept and go through them.

We live in a society where having emotions and be vulnerable seems something that needs to be fixed. I believe that vulnerability is the courage to be and with that we need to learn to honor our moments of sadness, respect our tears, and allow them to flow. We must allow the flow of whatever is in us out of respect for our Source, which is love, in order to keep our heart open. Only this way we can heal from our painful experiences and understand the whys of our pains, and where to go next and how to get there. It takes courage to face our emotions and our archaic emotional baggage. Suppressing emotions, and, ultimately, our inner Self, is a defense mechanism that only brings more suffering. The great wall of defense will not help keep away the pain, but will actually amplify it, while also preventing us from experiencing joy and the positive part of that experience…the growth!

How should we work with our emotions though? When I said recognize and observe your emotions, what does that mean? It means recognize for example that fear is there and talk to it.

Thank it for coming up, allowing you the choice to follow it or not. State that you won't go there. You have the choice to leave it there and take a different path. Recognizing fear gives us the privilege to choose a new and different path.

Remember:

> Recognize the emotion.
> Thank it for coming up.
> Make your choice and reach out for the alternative.

When we are sad, it's ok, sad is good, but we must allow this emotion to exist without fighting it, but embrace it. Let it pass, choose not to dwell on it but live it through it.

Our life is a tapestry of crossroads, obstacles, and having to climb walls, but the beauty of it is, we always have a choice. As human beings, we have the choice, and a new chance, to make our lives better every single sunrise. If we keep the heart open, we will know how to follow that woven path. It is woven for us, in our favor, not against us to trick us.

When emotions arise, especially when during moments of irritation or upset Breathing in and out allows us to stay in the moment, in the here and now, and does not allow us to space out to a future that is not yet, or a past that is "no longer". Practicing mindful meditation, this calming activity of deliberately breathing in and breathing out correctly, can help a great deal in practicing processing our emotions. Remember your daily moment of silence.

It's always a choice

Every life story is a tale that dwells in both halves of the glass. It's our choice, as narrator, to emphasize one of those halves, the positive or the negative. We can even choose to re-write our story as victim or victorious. It's a choice, only a choice.

I heard this story from a wonderful 83 year old woman. One day, when she was in her late 30s, exiting an elevator, she saw a young man whom she had been told wanted to get to know her. She was in a challenging moment of her life. As a single working mother of two she had her hands full with worries and she had no intention to make new acquaintances. She also realized of having closed her den and shut out the world. She was sad, terribly sad, and asking the Universe to show her the way. The young man said, "Hi. How are you? How is life treating you?" as soon as she heard that she recalled of wanting to automatically burst into a list of complaints, thankfully, when she realized what was happening, she decided this young fellow would meet her though knowing the best part of her life. Suddenly she made a radical turn with her narration she smiled, thought of her two children, and started describing what was great and precious in her life. When she was narrating this story with a vivid memory and enthusiasm, she emphasized that, with her surprise, the beautiful thing about that abrupt turn was that they were not lies. She said, "My affirmations were not an illusion or pretending to be anything they were not, but rather a realization that my glass was half-full. It was as if I had seen the fullness of the glass for the first time!" She added, she recited her life by the most painful end of it, but since then she consciously made an effort to put the good ahead in her life, whether she was thinking of it by herself or speaking to somebody. Has it ever happened to you to hear somebody referring to you and your life as fortunate or unfortunate? I have. Actually, I am often told how interesting or how unfortunate my life has been so far. Personally, I find it hilarious how we can put a positive or negative spin on things. We must understand that it is only the perception of the glass that is changing, not the glass or quantity itself.

Many times, we suffer and endure pain from actions that were done to us, other times we suffer from an imaginary pain, one we feel is from something done to us, but in reality, was never inflicted on us. We can become caught and frozen in those moments, creating a cage that will only prevent us from feeling positive emotions. We will fill up our days with what we do not like about something or somebody, and the space for what is beautiful in those people or those things will shrink. We will be only able to see and focus on the emptiness of the glass, completely blind and deaf to its fullness, living in a sleepwalking state and numbed to whatever could tickle our joy.

On a recent flight, I heard so many complaints. It is amazing and it has be amusing for me, to see how good we can be at choosing to make our days miserable. We are masters at self-inflicting misery, we have such a great talent and power for it. While riding an elevator in the airport with four other people, one man was complaining loudly to the rest of the passengers, visibly frustrated and upset about the slow speed of the elevator. He kept saying it was too slow, inflamed with rage and all he needed to do was get to his airline's lounge and relax before his next flight. Note: he only rode the elevator one floor up… Or a lady who refused to move her bag one space down from the upper compartment on the plane and complained about a guitar belonging to another passenger that was stored above her right in the space assigned to her seat. She grumbled the entire transoceanic flight…

The amazing and astonishing part of all this is that we choose to inflict this negativity from these kind of experiences on every single day of our life. Anger, rage, frustration, and resentment, to mention but a few, and whatever else. These are meaningless events, which anyway cover 75% or more of our daily routine, but even in more meaningful situation, the practice should be the same. Keep your heart open and everything will make sense. Everything. Even the most unwanted experiences, harsh incidents, or tests this life offers will make sense to you only if your heart is, and stays, open. Whatever unwanted event is happening, it too shall pass. The essence of life will be with you, and this one more experience will move you forward, closer to where you are supposed to go. In the midst of unwanted occurrences, try to stay focused on what matters. Hold onto the pain. In the daily life of bumps and obstacles, the stolen credit card, the flat tire on a rainy day…stay focused on what matters:

> Keep calm. Talk to your rising emotions.
>
> Be present. The knot will untangle. It will pass; it will end.
>
> Do not assume the future will be exactly like today. It will not.

Choose the victorious path, when the victim's path invites you in just consider making another turn. The victim's path is a trap that the ego itself lays out. If we fall into the trap we set ourselves up for a very miserable and sterile life where evolution is not happening, and only time goes by meaninglessly.

More often than we wish, we become tangled up in our own process of holding onto old resentments towards certain people in our lives. Often, we involve others in a tug of war against somebody else instead we should commit to teaching love and compassion, rather than mastering and teaching resentment. Resentment is only a toxic substance that poison our lives. Go beyond resentment, for it will not allow love to grow. It will only make its own wall grow higher, until it acts as a fortress. If we open our heart and teach love, since it is the vital and indispensable force in our lives we will then access more easily forgiveness, compassion, gratitude, acceptance without which life cannot be. Don't look for the reason to hate someone at any cost. Just let go... Rewrite the story. Refrain from labeling, judging, or resenting a person or circumstance or situation. Put your energies into the path of learning. Whatever happens to you, whether it be a nasty boss, a betrayal, unkind in-laws, it is there to teach you something. A failure is there for a reason. Do not push it away; go through it and learn. Always ask yourself, "What do I have to learn from this?" Most importantly, do not expect others to change. If you change first, everything will change around you.

"You must be the change you wish to see in the world.[7]"

— *Mahatma Gandhi*

CHAPTER 10

FINDING YOUR PURPOSE THROUGH INTUITION

Intuition is our true personal navigator, always conducting us in the right direction. Intuition is the device that translates our feelings, not emotions, into the road map to follow. Finding our purpose, our true calling, is a search that each of us can perform individually. Our personal choice is only between us and the Universe. Nobody can know our destiny, neither out of love, nor out of personal expertise on trends, statistics, or common sense. The more we feel passionate and driven to get closer to what we would like to do, the closer we will be in reaching our purpose. Let us learn to listen to our intuition even if it has a feeble voice, and in doing so we must be careful not to confuse it with impulses or instinct. When we use our intuition, all of our senses are at work. Most of us do not realize that intuition is the cable to directly communicate with the Universe, giving us the *power* to know, without fully understanding how we get to *know*. Intuition goes beyond intelligence and it is not polluted by reasoning, it is what surfaces directly from the heart. Conversely, an impulse is a mental stimulus triggered by an emotion, and instinct is a natural reaction that calls for quick response. When I refer to intuition, it's really what I define as "looking inside." The verb itself comes from the Latin *in* "inside" and *tueri* "look." If then we look deep into ourselves and listen, we will feel what is right for us while our mind will not be able to fabricate any "what ifs" or "buts," not tossing any doubts over it, and furthermore removing any obstacles. Following our intuition, we will feel confident, without contorted reasoning trying to convince us that it is wrong. No doubts or fears can last when we make a choice coming from our heart by listening to its whispers.

Our real job in this life is to find our calling, our purpose. Find it, honor it, and fulfill it. We tend to look far outside us, but it is really within us. The fact that we have dreams and aspirations is proof that the route to our purpose has been laid out, the reasons we are here has already been established. Frequently, instead of understanding the kernel of our dreams and moving forward towards it, we loiter, not honoring these aspirations. We interfere and inject rationality, creating a list of negatives: "I cannot do…" "This cannot be done," "Silly me, what am I thinking?" "I am a daydreamer." We even let others criticize us and our dreams. And there it is, the self-fulfilling prophecy.

Family members have cast premonitions on my future path, even out of love, as if I were a mold to be polished and refined by their intentions. However, I chose to listen to my truth—inside. I decided to listen to myself when my inner suggestions were in alignment with me. I learned to choose the voice inside which *I* felt was right. I elected to work, and work hard, not towards whichever path was easiest, but towards the path that resonated with my heart. I soon understood that although I was putting in a great deal of effort, I was not struggling against myself. I started to comprehend the difference between work, great effort, and struggle. When somebody would tell me to work harder on a task, if I felt it was true for me and it aligned with my path, I complied. Having someone's feedback is a gift if it is given out of love and genuine, positive feelings. Ultimately though, it's your voice that counts, that Divine voice within you. Despite the counseling and advice, we all may receive, we must acquire the ability to listen to the whispers of our heart, regrettably, nobody is teaching that to us. A good start however, is knowing what we do not want. It's absolutely fine to have no idea of where we want to go at times and what decision is best for us. The following points will guide you to intuitively know and acknowledge your purpose and the real reason for your journey *here*.

Know your personality and what stimulates your inner enthusiasm. What do you dream of doing? Enthusiasm means "divinely inspired" (from the Greek *entheos*).[8] Let the Divine that is in you inspire you.

Know your gifts and align them with your dreams.

Believe in your dreams. They are the clues, the lights shining over your path.

Ask for guidance in sharing your gifts with the world.

You matter. Take charge of your existence.

It is imperative to ignore our fears since failures *will* happen, but if we truly listened to our inner voice, they will be successful failures. They will be what I refer to as *Kairos*,[9] our moments of clarity…even if brought by pain, uncertainty, or deep and intense crises. The only way to not betray ourselves is to listen to our inner voice. Once we follow that voice towards our purpose we feel enthusiasm for life, filled with love for everybody and in everything we are doing. We will be living authentically, without having to negotiate with life, our choices will *feel* right, instead if we betray ourselves, we will feel depleted, drained of life's energy.

As with all facets of life, we might have to make some compromises along our path, but not to the point of renouncing what we know to be true. We must not compromise our true Self. It will be your choice, done out of love for something or someone but you will still be authentic to who you are. Each being is not born to be like someone else, but to be herself or himself because our existence matters to the Universe. Each of us has his/her own unique purpose; we are here with unique gifts to offer and to share.

Once we understand what we, as individuals were made for, there is no need to follow anybody else's footsteps and we can forge our own journey, without asking permission from anybody and without feeling pressure to emulate anyone. We will live feeling empowered even in tough times. Difficulties will remind us that we are working hard, but notice that we are not struggling, we are floating and swimming but not upstream, probably feeling tired, but not feeling like we are losing our lives over it. We will use fears, we will not allow them to block or paralyze us, but we will recognize that they are there, being brave enough to pursue our path anyway, using them to push us forward rather than stop us.

Do not be afraid. Dare to live, dare to push yourself forward, dare to choose your own path. If we see the step we took is wrong, the Universe will help us correct it. Paulo Coelho, in his book *The Alchemist*,[10] says that the Universe will plot to give you what you are planning and working to achieve.

Once you are able to align your spirit and soul through the seven inner abilities, you are wholly connected. Your soul and the Source will work together to bring about what you are ready to receive and synchronicity will occur. Whatever you need to achieve, or what you want, will show up in one way or another. When you have a desire, all you need is trust and the strength to pursue it. If a desire, based on the love and compassion you feel both for yourself and for others, comes up in you, it is a sign for that road to be taken. Remember things *will* come to your life when you are prepared to receive them. We need to keep meeting life as it comes and experience it. That is the truthful meaning of our journey, no matter what happens.

In reading these lines, know that a life in the light and love will contain both storm and peace, color and darkness. It is through these ups and downs, and only through them, that your soul's and spirit's evolution and growth are possible. Certain problems and grief will intensify and trigger the gifts within yourself. Often, during a limiting time in my life that was particularly filled with obstacles, I found that experience to open new pathways I could not help but follow. I would never have seen or taken these pathways if I had not let those constrictions and grief open my heart and my soul, winning over my fears and deciding to go in that direction.

Young women and young men need to understand the necessity of learning the skills to overcome those moments in such a way that each and every experience propels you forward into growth. Growth leads towards a better you and a better life, it is a great opportunity to grow up and evolve. My words in this book are designed to give you the tools and the skills to be able to carry your emotional baggage with serenity, without dragging it everywhere you go while rolling and collecting even more stuff on the way, becoming wiped out and drained by unwanted incidents. Rather, you will recognize that these skills will give the necessary "how-tos" to travel this journey of life peacefully and successfully.

There is no such a thing as an unfair Universe. The Universe is equipped with the right way for each of us. Accept what you are facing in any given moment because that moment is right for you.

When deciding becomes daunting

When emotions get in the middle it is very hard to follow the inner voice and we get confused and completely deaf and unable to recognize and listen to our intuition. Have you ever found yourself in situation when you have to make important decision but you do not know how and what and why you should go this or that way? One day is right and the other day for exactly the same amount and important reasons is left?

I have felt restless, devoured by fears and haunted by doubts. All the possible negative emotions overtook me and I could not do anything except be paralyzed, drowning in my own tears. Again, I asked my wise friend for help and he told me, "When you want to reflect your image in the water of a lake, and you cannot because the lake has rough waters, what do you do?" after some thinking I answered, "Ok, I guess I need to be still and wait for the water to calm down!" He smiled. I had no other option than to wait for the "stormy waters" of my emotions to settle down and know that everything would clear up. It was hard work, but I did it. I could see my image and the reflection of my surroundings in the water. Yes, now I could see clearly and I could make my decision. All we need to do in such a situation is to stay still and wait for our emotions to subside and our heart to rise.

Remember how precious you are

This of all, is my favorite recommendation: Do not let anybody demean you. Here is why.

When I was a teenager an uncle once told me that it would have been useless for me to continue my studies, since, he said, I would not have been able to achieve anything in life due the fact I apparently took after a family member whom he did not like. The cruelty of his words distressed my heart, as I loved him and never would have expected this dismissive attitude towards my goals and myself. While this inner pain was pervading me, I also heard my inner voice saying, "You are more than what he thinks." My voice inside told me that it was not true; I was more than what he thought, although my stomach ached and my breaking heart felt like a crystal cracking suddenly from top to bottom. Needless to say, what he said was very painful, hurtful, and not at all encouraging. But I decided to move forward. While my tears were soaking me and the fear of the future, a fear that my life would be difficult because of my choices, infused into my bloodstream, I heard a countering voice inside: "You are more than what he thinks" hammering inside my head. As a matter of fact, when I was studying in college and had moments of discouragement, well, believe it or not, thinking of what my uncle said gave me the strength to keep going. Remembering those hurtful comments reminded me of that voice: "You are more than what he thinks."

We must always remember that we are Divine creatures, more divine than what anybody thinks, more than what anybody tells us. Those unkind and wounding assertions come from someone's own fears, their own anger, their self-imposed limitations, their own frustrations. They are generated from other people's negative emotions. Just let them be. Free your life from any suggestions and comments that do not resonate with the whispers of your heart and the guidance of your soul. Let the whispers guide you; do not let the unresolved pain of others chisel your life into their predictions.

If we believe we are Divine creatures, none of those upsetting comments will ever truly influence our life. They may make us shake, doubt ourselves, or become fearful, but we will find the strength to follow our heart. We must never allow the echoes of those words to stick to the walls of our heart. They might hurt and they might make our heart bleed, but we must learn not to dwell on that. We must comprehend and believe our power gifted to us to unveil in a greater plan, which is greater than the negative individuals and greater than us. What they think, believe, and say is not a Universal truth. Nobody can derail us from the path arranged by the greater Source. Remember to stick with what matters, to stay focused on our intention to continue our life journey without proving to anybody that we are right, our inner voice will lead us to find the true path. If you are briefly thrown off the tracks by negativity, instead of following the provocation, go back to your track and work on achieving what you originally planned to achieve: peace, joy, or whatever it may be that you desired. It is as if you found your house suddenly on fire. Even if you saw who set the fire, is it worth your time to chase him? Or would your time be better spent in trying to put the fire out? Remember how precious you are.

Your Body, Your Temple

The body is a vehicle that allows our souls to complete this earthly journey and it is the temple where our own Divine resides. Mind, body, and spirit are a continuum, not three separate compartments. Therefore, to function well, they have to communicate well, and for that, they need to be treated well and properly taken care of.

I strongly recommend making positive and healthy choices and keeping them within easy reach, without the restriction of a disciplined system, those choices are much harder to embrace. We only need to create a daily environment for ourselves where we are constantly "tempted" by things that are good for us instead of being harmful: good food, good rest, good exercise, good habits. Once we set the beneficial surrounding, implementation will not be hard and the new lifestyle will run its course. For the new plan to become a sustainable lifestyle, our daily needs will need to mirror it. New small steps for a healthier and more conscious physical life, together with implementing these seven steps. It will bring about positive changes and it will result in enormous lifelong benefits.

CHAPTER 11

EPILOGUE

These days are full of conversation about manifesting what we desire, getting rid of our limiting beliefs, and using positive affirmations. These are useful and helpful activities, but if we do not align our souls with our desires and keep our connection with the Higher Source, we can spend our lives repeating affirmations that won't get us very far. Living by Love, Forgiveness, Compassion, Gratitude, Acceptance, Silence and Trust is essential to be able to align our soul with our desires and live a fulfilling balanced life in peace, joy, and happiness. All 7 steps should be practiced concurrently because:

> **Love** is the liaison to everything
>
> **Forgiveness** is the door to your heart
>
> **Compassion** is the ability to listen and be heard
>
> **Gratitude** is the mean to allow wonders
>
> **Acceptance** is understanding that the present is the only time you have
>
> **Silence** is the direct connection with the Source
>
> **Trust** is knowing you are always taken care of

Continue with these seven steps and embrace what life introduces in your path. Accept that your sister-in-law is not the one you wished for, nor is she the one you can have hoped-for conversations with. Accept that your brother does not understand certain things that are important to you. Your life's path is your own business, and so is theirs to them. Accept the way things are and do not be presumptuous in trying to change people. At first you will seem unable, but only through unconditional love, will this acceptance and change occur. Accept that they did not understand you when you most needed it, they could not. Whatever happens in any given moment, accept and surrender. Say yes to it.

Do not judge. Do not get frozen in your pain, in the cruelty of abuse, or in the pain inflicted on you. You are no longer in that moment. You only have the present, you *are* in the present. Be aware of what is frozen within you. Be brave and admit it; be braver and work on yourself. Only this way will you process those feelings and liberate yourself from them. Otherwise, they will discourage you forever and they will stick to you forever, preventing you from moving forward. The frozen pain will show up at your door stickier, heavier, and harder to get rid of. It will rule your life. So, be brave. Go within, dig and search for the work you "gotta do," and embrace it. Your life will be true and authentic. You will be whole only if you work on yourself. There is *no* such thing as being "completed" by somebody else; you are not a puzzle.

No suffering should be wasted, they are powerful opportunities for growth and evolution. Whenever something negative happens, it is too easy to blame someone else. Take ownership of the consequences that follow the choice you made, it most likely brought you where you are. The moment you accept responsibility, you have the power to change it.

Remember, every day, is a new opportunity. You have the power to decide who you are going to be every single day. Every morning when you wake up, you have the great opportunity to choose. How does it get better than this?

It is really my wish and hope that these few suggestions on living an awakened life can serve as guidelines to someone who comes across this book. Perhaps it can help them to skip some of the wrong turns I took.

I wish that once you have read these pages you gain an early recognition of your Divine worth and realize that you are never alone, even in the roughest of times. You will be able to feel it if you keep yourself connected to the Source through your open heart. I define "spirituality" as your own way to navigate the path of awakening. But when struggle hits, reflect upon the difference between struggle and effort. Personally, I still hold onto to my Christian beliefs and I ultimately came back to God, but with the conviction that He is my benevolent God, not the angry God of my childhood teachings. I encourage each of you to follow what you believe is true to your life path, may it be religion, self-love, or devotion to your future and aspirations. Even in the darkest moments, there is always a guiding light. Be assured that the darkness will not remain if you choose the light. Every human being has the potential to be awakened and live an awakened life, we must only choose—and allow— to be awakened.

RESOURCES

I feel compelled to pass on some recommendations for essential reading. These are books on the matter of life. By far, they come from voices with much more authority than mine.

Armstrong, Karen *Twelve Steps To A Compassionate Life*

Bach, Edward *Heal Thyself*

Chodron, Pema *Living Beautifully: With Uncertainty and Change, Start Where You Are: A Guide to Compassionate Living, When Things Fall Apart: Heart Advice for Difficult Times*

Chopra, Deepak *Buddha, A Story of Enlightenment, Reinventing the Body, Resurrecting the* Soul, The *Seven Spiritual Laws of Success*

Coelho, Paulo *The Alchemist*

Dyer, Wayne *The Power of Intention*

Gibran, Khalil *The Prophet*

Hesse, Hermann *Siddartha*

Judith, Anodea *Eastern Body, Western Mind: Psychology and the Chakra System As a Path to the Self*

Nepo, Mark *Seven Thousand Ways To Listen*

Nhat Hanh, Thich *Anger: Wisdom for Cooling the Flames, Answers from the Heart: Practical Responses to Life's Burning*

Questions, Fear: Essential Wisdom for Getting through the Storm, Present Moment Wonderful Moment

Tolle, Eckhart *A New Earth: Awakening to Your Life's Purpose, The Power of Now: A Guide to Spiritual Enlightenment*

Zukav, Gary *The Seat of The Soul*

The Bhagavad-Gita, Translated by Sir Edwin Arnold. Vol. XLV, Part 4. The Harvard Classics. New York: P.F. Collier & Son, 1909–14; Bartleby.com, 2001. www.bartleby.com/45/4/. [Date of Printout].

The Teachings of Mahatma Ghandi, Edited by Jag Parvesh Chander with a foreword by Dr Rajendra Prasad. The Indian Printing Works

The Holy Bible, New International Version (New York, 1978)

ENDNOTES

1. Gibran, Khalil. (2013) *The Prophet*. New York: Alfred-A-Knopf
2. Bach, Edward. (2009) *Guarire con i fiori (Heal Thyself)*. s.l. (Nuova IPSA)
3. Twain, Mark BrainyQuote.com, Xplore Inc., http://www.brainyquote.com/quotes/quotes/m/marktwain109919.html (accessed April 10, 2015).
4. Eckhart, Meister BrainyQuote.com, Xplore Inc., http://www.brainyquote.com/quotes/quotes/m/meistereck149158.html (accessed April 10, 2015).
5. Gibran, Khalil. (2013) *The Prophet*. New York: Alfred-A-Knopf
6. Tolle, Eckhart. (2004) *The Power of Now: A Guide to Spiritual Enlightenment*. s.l. Namaste Publishing.
7. Mahatma Gandhi, BrainyQuote.com, Xplore Inc., http://www.brainyquote.com/quotes/quotes/m/mahatmagan109075.html (accessed April 10, 2015).
8. Online Etymology Dictionary, Etymonline.com, http://www.etymonline.com/index.php?term=enthusiasm (accessed April 13, 2015).
9. "The right or opportune moment (the supreme moment)." Wikipedia.com, Wikimedia Foundation, Inc., http://en.wikipedia.org/wiki/Kairos (accessed April 13, 2015).
10. Coelho, Paulo. (1990) *El Alquimista (The Alchemist)*. Barcelona. Circulo De Lectores.

— thoughts & feelings —

— *thoughts & feelings* —

— *thoughts & feelings* —

— *thoughts & feelings* —

— thoughts & feelings —

— thoughts & feelings —

— *thoughts & feelings* —

— thoughts & feelings —

— *thoughts & feelings* —

— *thoughts & feelings* —

— *thoughts & feelings* —

— *thoughts & feelings* —

— thoughts & feelings —

― *thoughts & feelings* ―

— thoughts & feelings —

POWER HOUSE PUBLISHING

unleashing the power housed in you

Made in the USA
Lexington, KY
01 November 2017